0-DAYS-TO-EXPIRATION INDEX OPTIONS

Insanely Profitable

Trading Opportunities

XIAO GUDONG

TO

Susan, Angela, and Katherine

DISCLAIMER

This booklet discusses the zero days-to-expiration index as an asset class in the US financial market for educational purposes only. It is not an investment or trading recommendation and can not be construed as one.

TABLE OF CONTENTS

I always define my risk, and I don't have to worry about it because it's already defined.

Paul Tudor Jones

Uncover the Lucrative Potential and Unmatched Profitability of Zero-Days-to-Expiration Options.

If you are new to Zero-days-to-expiration options or 0-DTE, it is time to explore this insanely lucrative asset class.

But first, let's briefly talk about what exactly 0-DTE is.

CBOE first introduced S&P-500 index quarterly options in 1983. Due to its popularity, the quarterlies evolved into monthlies, and the weeklies started trading in 2005. At the beginning of weeklies, the contracts expire every Friday. Now, weeklies are expiring every day of the week. 0-DTEs are essentially the weeklies that are expiring TODAY.

Currently, only ten securities in the US market offer options contracts that expire daily; some are more liquid than others, with the S&P-500 index being the most traded security. There is also a mini version of SPX, the XSP. It is 1/10 the size of SPX. We will use XSP as the security of our choice throughout the following discussion.

Before diving into trading 0-DTE, let's empower ourselves with a brief review of two fundamental approaches to trading options: the short approach and the long approach.

I am sure you have read somewhere or heard from someone that TIME is the options seller's friend. It is true, but only in theory.

You see, the rationale behind selling options is that they are depreciating assets. Their value depreciates over time. Traders establish the short positions and theoretically buy them back sometime later at a lower price. The difference is the profit.

However, we also know that the volatility of the underlying assets makes holding short options positions dangerous.

Increased volatility makes stock price movements challenging to predict. It is precisely this unpredictability that inflates the value of options, calls and puts alike. The portion of the option's value affected by volatility changes is the time value, not the intrinsic value.

By extension, we can reason that the longer we hold on to our short positions, the more we are exposed to the danger of volatility.

The other profit or loss determining factor is the direction of the price movement. We profit if the price of the underlying goes our direction. We lose if the direction is against us. The price changes in the contracts are mainly related to intrinsic value. This is why sometimes the potential profit or loss can be much greater than the extrinsic part of the price. This is, of course, the sole reason why some traders choose the long side of the trade in the face of depreciating extrinsic value, as opposed to the short side.

So, when we decide to establish a position in options, we must consider both the extrinsic and intrinsic value of the contracts. However, neither of these two factors is under our control.

This is where so-called defined-risk strategies come in. Defined-risk strategies are simply hedge trades. We buy an options contract and sell a contract of another strike or a different expiration so that one of the contracts will benefit from the price movement, thus theoretically locking in our exposure.

Most spread trades, such as vertical spreads and calendar spreads, as well as more complex spreads like a butterfly or iron condor, fall into the defined-risk category. Traders can determine what their maximum risks are before the trades are executed.

The trouble with these defined-risk trades is that the maximum risks and profits are usually realized toward the end of the options' life; most of the time, it is at the expiration of the contracts, which could be days, weeks, or even months away. And there is no telling how the prices would fluctuate in the interim.

Here's where 0-DTE options shine. By trading 0-DTE, we take the reins on our exposure to time. The options expire the same day we enter the trade, so there's minimal time value in the options price, which significantly reduces price fluctuation due to sudden changes in volatility. It's like eliminating one of the two profit or loss factors from the equation. All we need to concentrate on is the direction of the underlying movement—akin to day-trading shares but with significantly higher leverage.

Needless to say, we can stay in the trade until it expires at market close, or if we have day trader status, we can exit the trades anytime before the markets close.

Let's Take A Closer Look

There are an infinite number of options and strategies in a broader sense. However, many of them involve time and time value. Those are not ideal strategies for 0-DTE, not just because there is only a limited amount of time value left on the last day of the options' life but also because the changes in the underlying index during the trading hours are most likely greater than the amount of the time value.

Due to this risk factor, we should completely rule out time-value-capturing singular short trade. As for directional trades, all singles, regardless of short or long, put or call, are fair games.

Another essential factor to consider is that there are only 6 ½ hours from start to finish to make a trade, enter, and exit; it is reasonable to expect a compacted price range for us to work in vis-a-vis a swing trade. We really do not have much time to wait for the trades to develop. And any three-or-more-legged strategies, such as iron condor and butterfly, may take longer to fill than we would like. Although we could divide these trades into two separate orders to complete the positions, it is another subject for another chapter.

This leaves us only two viable strategies: a singular long and a vertical spread. Please note that I have come to know other traders who are tremendously successful in trading exclusively butterfly and iron condors. I am not against it. As I have said, we can divide them into two separate trades to complete the setup.

In my experience, the volatility of the S&P index on most days varies between 18% and 20%. This means that a significant portion of a contract's price is still time value. There is no established pattern where the depreciation of time value starts to accelerate in a given day. However, the time value is usually diminished to a minuscule amount in the last two hours of the trading day..

Long calls, long puts, short calls, short puts, and vertical spreads are all directional trades, which means we need to get the directions right to win with them.

Does this mean trend-following strategies are more likely to win? Not necessarily. On a typical trading day, markets do not move straight up or straight down; they most likely zig-zag several times during the 6 ½ hours of trading. The same goes for bigger-scale trends; there will be down days in an uptrend and up days in a downtrend.

This does not imply that technical analysis is worthless in day trading. It is actually quite valuable in capturing the turning points of daily fluctuations. But at the end of the day, our gut feeling and luck play much more significant roles in determining our success in day trading than trades in larger trends.

Another crucial piece of information we need to gain bigger rewards is the range of the price movement. If we get the direction right, the bigger the price moves, the bigger our profit.

Some Logical Approaches

If we are convinced that what we talked about so far is all true, then the following trades make a lot of sense:

If we believe the index (SPX) will close higher than its open, we can enter an ATM one-strike spread right after the market opens at near 50 cents. It does not matter if it's long or short, put or call; they work mostly the same. We put 50 cents on the table, hoping to make the other 50 cents at close. Our loss is defined at around 50 cents, providing a sense of security in our trades.

The wisdom of this trade is that experienced traders can usually "feel" or make "analyzed predictions" of how the market would turn out at the end of the day.

And they are usually right. If that is the case for you, then you will have more winners than losers in the long run.

Or we can choose to enter a single put or call trade, long only. Our risk is defined, and our profit could be quite rewarding. But like most option trades, the further out-of-the-money, the bigger the profit and the cheaper the cost, but less likely to win.

The downside of the trade is that some extrinsic values will quickly evaporate depending on the fill time.

Long Call and Long Put

We have established that short single options trades should be avoided due to their inherited risks.

Long single options trades have a defined risk. As long as we deem the risk acceptable, successful trades could be very rewarding.

There you have it! 0-DTE does not have to be complicated.

But to win, we need to possess four things:

1. We need to have a lot of common sense
2. We need to have a proven-successful strategy,
3. We need to be ultra-discipline

4. and a little bit of luck.

As far as the market direction is concerned, there is really not all that much to analyze. We can all identify the direction of the price trend and reason about what is not likely to happen in the short term (a day or a few hours). Some knowledge of technical indicators helps, but too much technical analysis could trounce your common sense and your confidence.

Definitions of Basic Options Strategies

In case you are new to index and stock options trading and have never traded options except for covered calls. Here are the basic definitions or descriptions of the strategies mentioned in this booklet.

Single Trades: If we are long/short call or put contracts in one trading order, we are trading single options. Our cost, or the price of the contract includes both the extrinsic and extrinsic value.

Spread Trades: If in our order there is a long and a short of different strikes of the same expiration of the same underlying, it is a vertical spread. If the order consists of a long and a short of different expirations, it is a calendar spread. Most of these spread trades have a locked-in profit or loss, but not all. Spreads like "strangle" and "straddle" could have unlimited profit or loss potential, but the outcome could be very challenging to manage and are not suited for relatively volatility-stabled index options.

Butterfly: It consists of four or its multiples of contracts in three different strikes. Two contracts on the strike in the middle are long, two flanks are short.

Iron Condor: It is basically one set of put vertical spread plus one set of call vertical spread. There are no overlapping strikes. In other words, the four contracts are on different strikes.

The vertical spreads, the calendar spread, the butterfly, and the iron condor are all defined-risk trades. As their names imply, there are risks, but they are known.

Don't let anybody tell you there are zero-risk strategies. All options trades run a risk of losing money. What is essential to make money trading options is knowing where the risk lies and how to manage it.

Please remember that there is no free lunch in any financial market. Higher profits usually come with higher risks. This is especially true in the options market, where higher probability generally comes with lower profit.

Although this is my fourth year aiming to double my trading account by year-end, I am still making the same number of trades every day and constantly reminding myself that there could be some major flaws in my strategy that I have yet to discover.

Start Trading, This Is The Only Way To Learn

Having been trading and investing in the stock market for more than twenty years, Aside from my long-term shareholdings, I now trade exclusively 0-DTE for a living. I have developed a simple trading strategy that only requires about 1 ½ hours in the morning to put on the trades and ½ hours before bedtime to determine which contracts to trade the next day. I have doubled my trading account for three consecutive years before the start of 2024.

Most importantly, I do not adjusted the number of contracts in my orders to reflect the ever-growing size of my account. In other words, the number of contracts traded each day is consistent from the beginning of the year to the end.

You can do it, too. The couple of strategies that I use day in and day out are sensible and straightforward that they are literally boring. If I were to lay them out in front of you, you'd probably ask yourself, "Why didn't I think of it?" In fact, I have already given you the logic behind my strategies with this little booklet. Please read it again and put on a few actual trades, and perhaps you can craft your own trading strategies that are similar to mine or even better than mine.

Or you can read my strategy book which will be published in early August 2024.

Good Trading!

What Securities Offer 0-DTE Options?

- Nasdaq 100 Index (NDX)
- S&P 500 Index (SPX)
- Mini-SPX Index (XSP)
- SPDR S&P 500 ETF Trust (SPY)
- Invesco QQQ Trust (QQQ)
-

SPX has the highest trading volume among the above securities.

XSP is one-tenth the size of SPX.

Other securities may have 0DTE but they might not be available every trading day.